52 WORDS *that will* CHANGE YOUR LIFE

ALSO BY REGINA BRETT

Little Detours and Spiritual Adventures

God Never Blinks

Be the Miracle

God is Always Hiring

REGINA BRETT

52 WORDS *that will* CHANGE YOUR LIFE

...One Week at a Time

GRAY & COMPANY, PUBLISHERS
CLEVELAND

Gray & Company, Publishers
www.grayco.com

ISBN 978-1-59851-149-9
1

Contents

Contents

Contents

To Asher, Ainsley and River
my three joys

Introduction

You are going to have a great year.

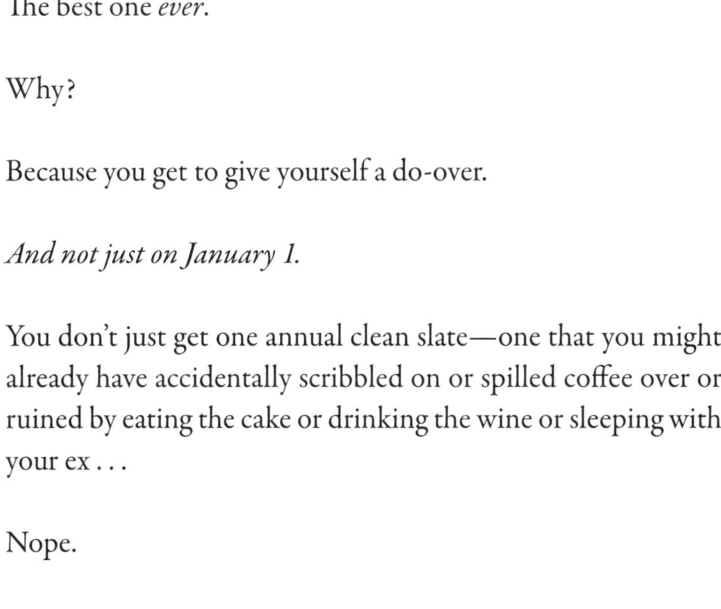

The best one *ever*.

Why?

Because you get to give yourself a do-over.

And not just on January 1.

You don't just get one annual clean slate—one that you might already have accidentally scribbled on or spilled coffee over or ruined by eating the cake or drinking the wine or sleeping with your ex . . .

Nope.

You get to start a new year *any time you want*.

Like right now.

A whole year is an awful lot to handle—especially at times when even one day can feel too much to manage. We're all short on time, all overwhelmed by too many to-do lists in our lives. There are so many parts of our lives we want to change, but at the end of the day, we just don't have the clarity, the time, or the energy to do it.

I wrote this book to lighten your load, not to add to it.

It offers 52 weekly "mini retreats" as a spiritual companion for those days when you feel lost and alone and just don't know where to start.

It's a mood booster. A thought replacer. A place to pause, to rest, to reset, to reboot, to refresh and start over.

Whether this is a good year or not is totally up to you. It doesn't depend on anyone else or on anything that happens outside of you. That's the beauty of it, the freedom of it, and the challenge of it.

Your great year is all about what happens inside you—one week at a time.

How to Use This Book

How to use this book?

The short answer: Any way you want to.

You can start from the beginning and let the book unfold naturally from 1 to 52. Or you can open it at random and trust that the page you land on is just what the Universe decided you needed this week.

You can kick it off at the start of a new year or birthday or make today the first day of the rest of your life and crack it open now.

This self-discovery reflection journal is a journey to more joy.

It's an interactive book, part me, part you. You will hear from me, and you will get to dig deeper within to hear from you. I hope my words lead you to listen to yourself because you truly are your own best guide on this journey called life.

You can carry this book in your purse, your briefcase, your glove box. Keep it on your nightstand and use it in your morning meditation or daily spiritual practice to start the day or end it.

You can breathe each word in and out in your daily meditation and all through the day when stress has a stranglehold on you.

This book is for you.

This book is for anyone who feels stuck and wants to start over but doesn't want to wait for a new year or even a new month to begin. It's for anyone who feels so confused, lost, or stuck about where to start that you just don't start at all.

You might be a college student or recent graduate who feels overwhelmed with the question: What's next? Or a parent stretched so thin that you feel crispy around the edges and the suggestion of self-care is too big a burden to add to all the people you're already caring for.

You might be someone who hates their job or loves it but feels burned out and bankrupt at the end of the day. Or someone whose dream died before it even sprouted. Or you feel like you blew it because your spouse bailed on you.

You might just be someone like me who constantly wants to improve themselves and find clarity to finish the soul journey we all came to Earth to complete.

As an archery coach, I tell archers to ignore the big outer rings of the target and just focus on the tiny X in the center of the target, the bull's eye. Each week, you focus on just one word. Each word is your center to aim for on the Target of Life. It might be *Joy* or *Hope* or *Courage* or something even better.

You don't have to put yourself through another grueling 100-day boot camp or 40-day fast or 30-day challenge to try (and fail) to change your life.

All it takes is one word. One word has the power to change your life. One word is all it takes to turn you into a Guardian of the Galaxy or a Jedi knight or a more mindful human being or all three.

One word is a compass point. A reset button. A trail marker to get you on the right path.

You can turn this book into your weekly reflection or daily discovery journal. You can turn it into your prayer partner or your courage companion.

No matter how you use it, make it an adventure. Something you look forward to, not something you dread. It's an invitation to grow happier, calmer, clearer.

Here's what's tucked inside. For every week you get . . .

One word each week

I love words. I love that in the Bible the Gospel of John starts with these words: "In the beginning was the Word, and the Word was with God, and the Word was God." Wow. That's how powerful words are.

This book gives you one word to ground you in the present moment. You can use it as a focal point to get you through anything life hands you. When I went through Lamaze training years ago to endure childbirth with no painkillers, I chose a focal point on the wall to stare at to get through each contraction. I carried that focal point practice through life to get me through cancer treatments that included surgery, chemotherapy, and six weeks of radiation.

Instant gratification

Once you have completed the word and the activities that go with it, check off each completed word in the Table of Contents so you can get that boost of instant gratification. High-five yourself and get ready to move on to the next word.

A brief quote to inspire you

These are words from me that became compass points in my own life, words that life sent me to get me through childhood trauma, recovery from alcoholism and cancer, and the end of my 29-year marriage.

A short reflection to guide you

These are words that have centered me and challenged me and changed me over the past six decades. They come from my own life experiences. I want you to have something test-driven that I know works because I've worked it.

A simple yet challenging question to ask yourself through the day

Albert Einstein once said if he had an hour to solve a problem and his life depended on the solution, he'd spend the first 55 minutes determining the proper question to ask, then he could solve the problem in less than five minutes.

Each week you get one question to carry around in your heart to stir up holy curiosity. Pose the question to your soul, then listen for the answer in whatever happens that week or in the stillness around whatever is happening.

An affirmation to center you all through the day

An affirmation is like setting an intention for the day. It's a way to declare the truth and Truth about who you are and who you are becoming. Even if you don't believe it, say it aloud until you do. You can use it like a mantra to chant over and over to stop the noise of doubt in your head and silence all those intrusive thoughts.

An action to change you

If you're like me, you spend a lot of time planning your life to avoid taking the next right step that would actually change your life. I'm giving you just one action to take each week. Just one. You can add more, but don't pile them on and turn this into boot camp or an endless to-do list that wears you out and keeps you running from yourself. Nike had it right: *Just do it*. And just do one.

A writing prompt to discover more of your own inner guidance

Don't let the prompts intimidate you. Just move your pen or pencil along and don't stop to edit. No correcting grammar or punctuation while you're writing. That would be like driving a car with the emergency brake on. You aren't going to get very far. The goal is completion, not perfection, because you're already completely perfect.

You already have all the answers you need deep inside you.

What else? You get to fill the book with your hopes and hallelujahs, your doodles and dreams, your wishes and wonder.

Create connections with others

This book material has a copyright, but I encourage you to take screenshots of the pages you might want to carry in your phone to get you through the day. You can even text a quote to a friend to give them a boost. I'd love to see what you create, so share yours on TikTok, YouTube, Facebook, Instagram, etc. Be sure to #ReginaBrett52 and tag me @ReginaBrett.

Build community

Create an inspirational community for yourself with a book club or writing group or prayer chain.

Create a text thread with your friends, family, prayer group, or book club members to share reflections about each word.

Share insights about it at the dinner table to spark discussion with your family. Use the questions or writing prompts to discover more about them.

Buy a copy for your pastor, priest, or rabbi to share to inspire others.

No matter how you choose to use what's in this book, know that this book chose you.

You are ready to start.

I'll be with you every week, in every word, cheering you on this great adventure called life. Let's get going!

— Regina

52 WORDS

Breathe

Breathe. It calms the mind.

Breathing is the most essential thing we do to stay alive. It takes absolutely no effort. Our body does it without any struggle. We do it mindlessly, but imagine the power of each breath if we took them in mindfully.

They say you can go three hours without shelter in extreme weather, three days without water and 30 days without food, but you can only go three minutes without oxygen.

Close your eyes and feel your lungs expand and contrast as slowly as you can. Just inhale . . . *one, two, three,* hold . . . *one, two, three*, and exhale slowly . . . *one, two, three*. . . Let your breath slow you down and silence all the noise in your head.

Whenever fear or anxiety creeps in, whenever you hear bad news or feel disappointed by life, pause and breathe in the words, "All is well, all is well, all is well." Because it is.

Question

When I hold my breath, what am I resisting?

Affirmation

My breath connects me to all the power there is, to all the power I need, to all the power I am.

Action

For one minute every day, I will pause and be mindful of the very breath I take in and out. I will send that breath to my heart to wrap it in a pillow of peace. I will breathe in love, peace, calm, comfort, and joy. I will exhale fear, shame, grief, anger, and anxiety so I can inhale more gratitude.

Discovery

As I write, with each breath I exhale all my . . .

....

....

....

....

....

....

....

....

....

....

....

....

....

Aim

Align yourself first. Then take action.

In times of inner or outer turmoil, everything can feel like a moving target I can't hit. So much changes so fast, and not everything lands back in place.

But one thing was and is always clear for me: the aim of my life.

That tiny X in the center of my Target of Life remains the same.

In archery, I never aim for the outer rings. No archer does. Those outer white rings are bigger and easier to hit, but you only get 1 point for landing an arrow in the largest ring. If you hit that tiny X in the middle, you score a perfect 10. That's where you aim to send your arrow in every shot you take.

The X in my Target of Life is me and God. No one else. That's my aim every day, to spend time in meditation and prayer with this power that is Love so the rest of the day unfolds with clarity and ease.

God rarely hands me the blueprint to my week, but God daily gives me clarity to take the next, clear, simple, right step.

When you're feeling scattered, aim for your X and forget the rest.

Question

What is my X, my number-one focus in life that never changes?

Affirmation

In the quiet of my soul, I calmly and clearly hear the next step to take.

Action

I will draw a target of circles and put me and God in the center.

Discovery

Here's what it would take to make joy a priority in my life . . .

....

....

....

....

....

....

....

....

....

....

....

....

....

Forgive

Forgive everyone everything.

It's time to set yourself free.

Holding on to resentments keeps us tethered to that person and that pain forever. It's like we locked ourselves in prison with them. It's like we drank the poison we hoped would hurt them. Yikes!

Imagine what would happen if we set all the captives free? All the hostages from our past? Our parents, siblings, exes, children, bosses, coworkers. What if we freed them all?

Forgiveness doesn't mean we have to become best buddies with them or spend holidays together or invite them to our book club. It means we free that person from the horror story we keep retelling ourselves, a story that continues to haunt and hurt us, not them.

Tell yourself a new story. Give yourself a new ending, a happy one, with no victims and no villains. Everything really does happen *for* you, not *to* you. Tell that story.

Question

What do I gain by holding people hostage?

Affirmation

When I forgive others, I also set myself free. Today I will open the channel to let more Love flow into my life and more Love to flow through me and onto the world.

Action

I will forgive three people this week, including myself. I will write the old story down, then write down a new story. Then I will burn the old story and release it forever.

Discovery

It's time to forgive myself for . . .

....

....

....

....

....

....

....

....

....

....

....

....

....

Now

Burn the candles, use the nice sheets, wear the fancy lingerie. Don't save anything for a special occasion. Today is special enough.

I'm tempted to buy a watch that tells time in one word: *Now.*

The only time we really have is right now.

We spend way too much time rehashing and replaying the past like a home movie that doesn't end well, or we fast-forward into a future that scares the pants off us.

I spend way too much time and energy clinging to yesterday and dreading tomorrow. I miss out on the precious present that is waving hello to get my attention.

We're missing so much wonder. Let's turn off the cell phone for a while and stop using Facebook, Twitter, TikTok, Instagram, and Snapchat to escape the moment we're in. This is a beautiful, special, unique, soon-to-vanish-forever-from-the-face-of-the-Earth moment. Don't miss it.

The only time we have is right now, this moment. Don't skip it. Savor it. This special day was delivered to you from the Universe. This day is a gift. Open it.

Question

What keeps me from being fully present in this moment?

Affirmation

In the present moment, all is well, always.

Action

Tape the word Now *on your phone, mirror, and dashboard this week to remind yourself to be present.*

Discovery

The present moment is inviting me to discover . . .

....

....

....

....

....

....

....

....

....

....

....

....

....

Bravery

Bravery takes practice.

My cell phone has different ringtones to match my mood and my callers.

Most days it plays the *Star Wars* "Cantina Band" happy music. For my daughter, it plays Pachelbel's Canon. For another family member, it plays, "Shut up and dance with me."

On days when I need a bravery boost, it belts out, "I wanna see you be brave" by Sara Bareilles.

I call it bravery practice. I do it whenever fear tries to stop me.

As a child, I had a bad experience going to a dentist who never used painkillers. I got a new dentist but am sometimes still scared to go, so I look in the mirror and tell myself, *Today I get to practice being brave.*

If you practice being brave, then bravery will become your automatic response to fear. You won't leap tall buildings in a single bound or lift a screeching locomotive off the railroad tracks, but you will be able to free the spiders from the bathtub and walk around in the dark without a flashlight.

If you need to, find a Bravery Buddy, someone braver than you. Together, conquer one thing that still scares you. Practice being brave together.

Question

What is bravery asking of me in this moment?

Affirmation

I'm not afraid of the storm. I am the storm.

Action

Tuck yourself in with a bedtime story of a time when you were brave.

Discovery

My biggest acts of bravery so far in this lifetime have been . . .

....

....

....

....

....

....

....

....

....

....

....

....

....

Ask

If you don't ask, you don't get.

My former spouse taught me long ago, "If you don't ask, you don't get."

He was the king of asking and getting. Upgrades on airlines. First-row seats at concerts. Discounts at stores.

Asking always makes me feel vulnerable, but it's like a muscle: The more you use it, the stronger it gets. So I've learned to ask away. Sometimes people say no and life gives me a great workout that I don't want, but it definitely makes me stronger.

Start off small and ask for things and for help that is easy for someone to give. Then once a week, make a big ask. Ask, but pause first to ask yourself: Is this the right person to ask? Are they supportive? What do I need? What do I want?

You won't always get what you want, but if you don't ask, you never will.

Even if you don't get what you want, you spoke up and asked, so you *did* get something you want—a more powerful you.

Question

What is the one thing I need to ask for right now?

Affirmation

The simple act of asking empowers me to attract all the help I need.

Action

List three people who are most likely to help me if I do ask.

Discovery

I am finally ready to speak up and ask for . . .

Listen

You learn a lot more when you listen.

In recovery programs where people are trying to get sober, the old timers tell the newbies, "God gave us two ears and one mouth so we would listen twice as much as we talk." And this: "Take the cotton out of your ears and put it in your mouth."

I still talk way too much. Sometimes I'm so busy forming my response or my answer, I'm not truly hearing my daughter or friends or grandkids. I'm not listening all the way through. I'm also guilty of interrupting people to give them advice they didn't ask for. I cringed when a friend told me, "When you give advice no one asked for, that's actually criticism." Ouch. Guilty as charged.

Listening is learning. If you're the one doing all the talking, you aren't learning anything new from life.

Everyone and everything can teach us if we listen. Even the birds, the crickets, and the purring cat have something to teach us.

Question

How does it feel to really be heard?

Affirmation

My life is full of holy messengers. I am ready to be silent and hear what they have to say.

Action

Every time someone speaks to me, I will make eye contact and heart contact and listen all the way through before I open my mouth to speak.

Discovery

I need to listen more to . . .

....

....

....

....

....

....

....

....

....

....

....

....

....

Thanks

Gratitude turns whatever you have into a blessing.

Cancer was one of my greatest teachers.

Cancer taught me to never take one single day for granted. All these years later, every morning before I get out of bed, the first thing I do is give thanks. I thank God for another day of life. No matter what will or will not happen, I'm here and alive to see it all unfold. That's a great start to any day.

Then I give thanks for all the people in my life, my inner circle that includes my children, their spouses, my three grandchildren, and my dearest friends.

At the end of the day, the last thing I do is to give thanks for the day. No matter what did or didn't happen, I'm still here, and that's miracle enough for me.

Sometimes I pray, "Dear God, thank you for all you've given me. Thank you for all you've taken from me. Thank you for all that you left me with." The Jesuits taught me to pray, "Your love and Your grace are enough for me."

They always are.

Question

How can I thank this moment right in front of me?

Affirmation

Thank You for my very being because I love being me.

Action

I will start and finish every day by saying Thank You, *no matter what happens in between.*

Discovery

There is so much to love about my life, starting with this . . .

Comfort

Adjust your own oxygen mask
before helping others
or you'll be of no use to anyone—
including yourself.

Before we can comfort others, we need to comfort ourselves.

You have nothing to give others if you don't fill yourself back up. Too many of us give away every ounce of our time and energy to others and end up exhausted, bitter, and resentful.

It's time to change all that. Climb into your comfort zone for a little while every day and nurture yourself. Rest your weary soul. Take a nap, read a poem, light a candle. Eat some comfort food. A dish of ice cream. A fresh nectarine. A bowl of raspberries.

If you don't have a comfort spot, create a nest, a special place in your home where you can go and be at peace. Cover a night-stand with a beautiful place mat. Set a vase of flowers by the bathtub. Create a refuge no one can take away.

When I travel abroad, I often place a scarf and photos of the people I love on the nightstand. Then I play a favorite song, with Garth Brooks or Adele singing, "Make you feel my love."

Question

What is the most comforting thing I can give myself right now?

Affirmation

Comfort is a gift I must give myself before I can give it to others.

Action

Create a sanctuary where you can pray or dream or create. Hang some plants or art, or set out your favorite poetry, pottery, or books.

Discovery

My future self is urging me to . . .

....

....

....

....

....

....

....

....

....

....

....

....

....

Meditate

Consult your own soul. Deep inside you already have all the answers you need.

The most important thing you can do every single day is meditate.

Most people offer all sorts of reasons not to meditate: It's too boring. Too difficult. Too complicated. Too spiritual. Or they simply don't have the time to meditate.

Meditation actually *gives* you more time. We've all heard the saying, If you're too busy to meditate, you're too busy. St. Francis de Sales once said, "Every one of us needs half an hour of prayer a day, except when we are busy. Then we need an hour."

Prayer is talking to God; meditation is listening. I pray and ask for help and blessings for others and give thanks, but meditation is when I simply sit at the feet of a Higher Presence and open my heart.

Just do it for a few minutes and it will give you hours of clarity as your day unfolds. Do it daily every morning and every evening, and everything in your life will change. Everything.

You will find a new clarity that finds you all through the day. It will guide every decision, every choice, every interaction.

At first it will churn up all kinds of noise and nonsense. I've been doing it almost daily for forty years and some days it feels like my brain is trying to kill me. But if you sit in silence long enough and often enough, the noise floats away like a cloud, and you start to live from a deep peace, the kind that surpasses all understanding.

Question

What is my biggest resistance to meditation?

Affirmation

With every breath, I breathe in love and breathe out peace.

Action

I will carve out at least five minutes every day to sit quietly and greet the peace inside me.

Discovery

Here's what my life would look and feel like if I meditated on a regular basis . . .

....

....

....

....

....

....

....

....

....

....

....

....

....

Love

All that truly matters in the end is that you loved.

The Beatles got it right: All you need is love. It really is that simple.

Many years ago I dumped all my spiritual confusion, life problems, and daily woes into the arms and heart of a beautiful soul, a Jesuit priest named Joe Zubricky. I had showed up at the Jesuit Retreat House in Parma full of anger at God and confusion over faith and life in general. What exactly did God want from me? What was God's will for me? I felt so lost and alone.

Father Joe simply smiled and said, "At the end of our lives, God will only ask one question. Just one. 'Did you love?'"

That question haunts me and shapes every day I'm in ever since he gave it to me as a gift back in 1981.

I'm not waiting until the end of my life to give that question an answer. At the end of every day I ask myself, "Regina, did you love today?" Then I check my heart. Did I close it on anyone?

If so, tomorrow is another opportunity to love.

To love God, to love me, to love every person who shows up on my path today, especially the person right in front of me.

Question

Who needs my love today?

Affirmation

I love myself, my life, and everyone in it.

Action

I will thank the person who has loved me the most in my life, then I will give myself a hug and love me so I can love everyone else better.

Discovery

I know I am loved. Here's the proof . . .

Play

Instead of building a stronger work ethic, strengthen your play ethic. It's time to fit more fun into your life.

Life is supposed to be fun.

Even amid all the sorrow shared in recovery rooms, people often quote this passage from the Big Book of Alcoholics Anonymous:

"We are not a glum lot . . . We absolutely insist on enjoying life . . . We think cheerfulness and laughter make for usefulness . . . We are sure God wants us to be happy, joyous, and free."

It took a long time and many retreats for me to believe that God delights in me and truly wants me to be happy, joyous, and free. The shift happened at a retreat at the Abbey of Genesee when I prayed with the monks from their book of Psalms: "And I will come to the altar of God, the God of my joy."

Joy. We are called to joy. Not every single minute of every day, but every single day should have some element of fun in it. Joy is our birthright.

When was the last time something made you smile for hours or laugh so hard that you spit out your coffee or almost peed your pants?

If you can't figure out how to have fun, create a Fun Team. Go through your phone or Facebook friends and create a team of the most joyful people in your life, the ones who aren't afraid to laugh loudly and often.

Life is short. Play hard.

Question

What would happen if I made play a priority?

Affirmation

Joy is my birthright.

Action

I will create a Fun Team of 5-10 people to go on playdates and adventures. I will go on one this week.

Discovery

I am the happiest when . . .

Grow

Give birth to yourself as often as needed.

Inside every seed, no matter how big or small, is the promise of an oak tree or a zinnia or a zucchini.

All that life might rest dormant inside that tiny seed for a while, even for years, but the tiniest seed carries within it the code for a beautiful life. That grand, mystical DNA offers a blueprint for bigger and better things.

So do you.

But you can't reach for the sky without planting roots in the dirt. When you feel mired in the muck and mess of life, don't fight it. Don't resist. Don't try to dig your way out. Sink into the mud. Relax into the mess. All that crap is fertilizer for your new life. You are getting ready to give birth to a new you.

The next time you see an acorn or an angel-winged maple seed, hold it up next to a massive oak or maple. Then imagine the power of all that DNA in every cell of yours that is just waiting to sprout, to use every talent, to launch every dream.

Give yourself this pep talk: Ready? . . . Set? . . . GROW!

Question

What's the biggest obstacle that keeps me from growing a more abundant life?

Affirmation

I am ready, willing, and able to grow a richer, bolder, more abundant life.

Action

This week I list my fears on paper and release them to the Universe.

Discovery

I am so ready to grow into a new me and change the way I . . .

....

....

....

....

....

....

....

....

....

....

....

....

....

Soar

It's up to you to launch your life.

I love to fly.

The first time I ever flew was at the county fair when I was 10. My dad asked the pilot for a discount to send a handful of his 11 kids on a helicopter ride. He didn't have much money, but Dad flew 38 missions as a tail gunner in WWII and wanted us to see the world from the air. I loved sitting in that chopper hovering over the entire fair, seeing God's grand view of the world.

Decades later, I took a doors-off helicopter ride over an active volcano in Hawaii. How wild to see the inside of the earth and that bubbling, glowing, orange lava inside Mauna Loa.

I'm never afraid to get on a plane. Before I board, I touch the metal of the plane's entrance, pause, and bless the pilot, the plane, and everyone on it.

Most times I say, "Either get me to my destination safely or take me Home quickly." Then I surrender the outcome to a God who loves me.

Too many of us live our lives on the tarmac. We're too afraid to take off. Or we're in a holding pattern, making the same boring circles over and over.

Fear keeps us grounded: What if there's turbulence? What if I get sick? What if I fall?

Ah, but what if you soar?

Question

What is keeping my life stuck on the runway?

Affirmation

Life, I am ready to soar higher than I ever imagined. I am ready for takeoff!

Action

I will draw a boarding pass to where I want my life to go.

Discovery

My ideal life involves lots of . . .

No

When it comes to getting what you want in life, don't take no for an answer.

No is such a small word but carries so much power when you actually use it.

Saying *no* protects our life force and our energy. Saying *no* doesn't make us mean; it makes us clearer about what we need and want from ourselves and others and from our lives.

I'm usually afraid to let others down by saying *no*, so I let me down instead and end up drained or hurt. My big fear is that I'll be rejected by someone else's future *no*. I'm also afraid the person I say *no* to will feel rejected. Too often I disappoint me so I won't disappoint them.

No is your ticket to *Yes*. *No* is your holy guardrail when used the right way. It will keep you from crashing from exhaustion. You have to decide what to say *no* to so you can trim out all the clutter from your calendar and your home and your soul and every relationship that drains the life out of you.

No is the permission slip I give myself to live the most vibrant, joyful, exciting life I have been called to live.

Question

What will I say No *to today so I can say* Yes! *to me?*

Action

I will practice saying the word No *at least five times a day, even if it's just to the mirror.*

Affirmation

No *is a holy word that creates an opening so that I can say a holier* Yes.

Discovery

If I had just six months to live, here's what would I say No *to so that I could say* Yes *to life . . .*

Simplify

Get rid of anything that isn't useful, beautiful, or joyful.

"Simplify, simplify, simplify."

Henry David Thoreau was right, although his buddy Ralph Waldo Emerson believed that one "simplify" would have sufficed.

The details and duties of life can weigh us down. Physical clutter can overwhelm us. I declutter my closets and cupboards often, but I sometimes feel buried under an avalanche of paperwork and projects in my office. I'm learning to let most of it go in the recycle bin and to stop saying *yes* to every request for my time, talent, and energy.

You are allowed to release what no longer serves you. That might mean doing a digital detox, too. Delete apps, podcasts, or playlists that no longer serve you.

Donate those clothes and shoes you don't wear. They might be someone else's best outfit. It might also be time to donate those dishes you inherited from your grandmother that you never loved or to stop doing all those traditions every holiday that just add stress to your life.

Less is more. Create more time and space for people and things that fill you up instead of draining you.

Question

What's the payoff for holding on to so many things that don't bring me joy?

Affirmation

My life sparkles with joy when I trim it down to the essentials.

Action

I will get rid of seven things this week that aren't useful, beautiful, or joyful.

Discovery

This is what a simpler life looks and feels like to me . . .

Dance

Dream with your feet. Dance.

Constanze Mozart was so enchanted by her husband's music that she proclaimed, "Dancing is like dreaming with your feet."

They always say, "Dance like no one is watching." That's the only way I can dance. I usually pretend I'm invisible, that no one is watching my awkward moves. Or if I'm home, I turn out the lights and crank up Queen singing, "Don't stop me now," and nothing stops my feet and hands and hair from flying.

I go country line-dancing as often as my daughter lets me join her at the Dusty Armadillo. I can't always follow the moves of everyone around me, but when my cowboy boots hit that dance floor, I'm more alive than ever. As long as I don't step on any toes, I'm dancing well enough for me.

I'm relieved that someone is watching because the veterans gently point a finger indicating which direction we're going next so I don't bump into someone and cause a domino of fallen cowboys.

Dancing connects your body, mind, and spirit to create a joyful celebration. Who cares what anyone else thinks of your party?

To dance is to use your wings, the ones on your heart that allow you to soar.

Question

What keeps me from celebrating being in my body?

Affirmation

Every time I dance, I celebrate being in this beautiful body.

Action

I will dance to one song this week, no matter who is watching.

Discovery

Here's what my life would look life from the aerial view with me soaring in it . . .

Sing

Every bird has a song. So do you. The world is waiting to hear it.

Saint Augustine said, "To sing is to pray twice."

Whether you talk to God every day or are no longer on speaking terms, you can always sing to lift your spirit to a higher energetic plane.

I love to sing. I sing in the shower, in the car, and often catch myself singing in stores. I laugh when people stare and whisper. Who cares? They can sing along with me if they want to.

Even if you sing off key, sing anyway. Sing louder. It will still be music to God's ears. Give your feelings a voice. Sing out your sadness. Sing out your loneliness. Sing out your anger. Sing out your fear.

I've also discovered the power of singing bowls and sound baths. I once attended an eight-part sound bathing series to clear the seven chakras. A woman unpacked various sizes of white quartz bowls and gently tapped or swirled a mallet along the edges to produce various sound waves that felt glorious. Each bowl sang to me and through me. They felt like wind chimes for the soul.

Sound waves carry a powerful energy that can smooth and heal those ragged edges inside and leave you feeling cleansed and ready for new energy to flow through.

Question

What do I love most about my voice?

Affirmation

My voice is a rare, unique, beautiful gift that brings me and others joy.

Action

I will make a playlist of the soundtrack to my life and sing along.

Discovery

These songs always give me comfort and make me feel at home in myself . . .

....

....

....

....

....

....

....

....

....

....

....

....

....

Miracles

If you want to see a miracle, be the miracle.

Albert Einstein gave us two choices in how to live our lives. Just two.

One of the most brilliant men who ever lived said, "There are only two ways to live your life. One is as though nothing is a miracle. The other is as though everything is a miracle."

I don't understand his theory of relativity, but I do understand that simple choice, and I'm going with the answer that includes everything.

My friends in recovery often quote this line from their Big Book: "We had to fearlessly face the proposition that either God is everything or else He is nothing. God either is, or He isn't. What was our choice to be?"

Again, I'll take everything.

I often remind myself of that motto, "Don't quit before the miracle happens." I add this to it: Don't quit *after* it happens because there are always more miracles to come.

We're surrounded by miracles. Want to see one? Just look in the mirror.

You—yes, you—are a miracle.

You're also a miracle catcher. You have the power to notice them, gather them up, bury your face in them, inhale them, then toss them like confetti into a world hungry for more miracles.

Question

Where am I called to be the miracle for someone today?

Affirmation

I am a miracle who is worthy of more miracles.

Action

Every time I see my reflection today, I will smile back and give thanks for the miracle of me.

Discovery

The last time I was touched by a miracle . . .

Clarity

When in doubt, just take the next right step.

I often remind myself whenever I'm confused or overwhelmed, "Regina, all you have to do is take the next right step. That's all." That's always enough.

There's always one clear step. It usually isn't a big leap. Most big leaps can be broken down into a dozen steps that most of us are too scared to take. Just take one of them and the next step will be revealed, along with the courage to take it.

Too often I want to wait until I see the grand blueprint unfold before I'll agree to the next small step. Life doesn't work that way. It's a mystery, and that's a good thing. If we saw the whole chapter or book unfold, we'd be too scared to turn the page.

If I don't get enough clarity for one right step, I ask for it. And if I miss it, I use my Secret Weapon Prayer:

"Dear God, I need the kind of clarity only You can give. I've prayed for it and listened but am still lost and confused. I have faith in your great love for me so I must have missed the clarity you've already sent. Please be more obvious. Send me a spotlight, a sledgehammer, or a billboard."

God usually bonks me over the head and sends all three.

Question

What single small step do I know with clarity to take right now?

Affirmation

I already have all the answers I need inside of me.

Action

I will take inventory of that which is clear and take the next right step.

Discovery

This is what's keeping me from taking the next small step I know I need to take in my life . . .

Bold

Be eccentric now. Don't wait for old age to wear purple.

Life shouldn't feel like homework. Sadly, for too many people, it does. Henry David Thoreau said, "The mass of men lead lives of quiet desperation." Women, too.

Work feels like drudgery. Relationships feel boring. The future scares us into doing nothing to change today. We end up stuck in a rut. And the difference between a rut and grave? There's a bit more room to move around.

Helen Keller, who had every reason to sit on her butt and do nothing but complain, said: "Life is either a daring adventure or nothing at all."

Make it an adventure. Give yourself reasons to say *yes* to life, not more excuses to say *no*. Living is too dear to miss out on.

Sure, you might get hurt, but so what? If you do, it's a great story you get to tell for the rest of your life and add to your Bravery Résumé.

"Whatever you can do or dream, begin it," as Goethe said. "Boldness has genius, power, and magic in it."

Make today a wild, bold adventure. And you're never too old to be bold.

Question

What keeps me from owning my bold, beautiful self right now?

Affirmation

I am fearless. I am bold. I am brave.

Action

List five bold adventures to take, and schedule one on the calendar.

Discovery

I love this vibrant, bold version of me . . .

Hugs

The world and everyone in it could use a great big hug.

A good hug squeezes the stress and sorrow right out of you.

My Slovak gramma gave the best hugs. It was like being wrapped in a big, soft pillow. I can still feel myself in her arms, even though she died decades ago when I was 19. My favorite place was inside her hug.

My mom was too busy to wrap us up in hugs. There were 11 of us hungry for affection, and she was worn out. I used to love emptying the clothes dryer for her. I'd open it as soon as the machine stopped so I could hold all those warm, clean clothes in my arms, hug them to my heart, and let that warmth fill my body and my soul.

Scientists have found that hugging relaxes you by releasing oxytocin, a chemical they call the "cuddle hormone."

Yes, hugging really does make you feel happy, whole, and less stressed.

Hugging comforts both the person giving it and the person receiving it. A hug makes you feel safe, like you're home no matter where you are in the world. The person hugging you claims you worthy of love, and you feel less alone.

The next time someone hugs you, savor it and let them be the first to let go.

Question

Where can I get or give a hug today?

Affirmation

Every hug I give and receive fills me and others with great love.

Action

This week I will hug something or someone every day: a person, a tree, a stuffed animal, or me.

Discovery

Here's the person who gave me the best hugs — and what made them so special . . .

Nature

Get outside every day. Miracles are waiting for you to discover.

When my head and heart feel like they are spinning out of control on all the *what ifs* that might happen but probably never will, I go outside to ground myself on the Earth. Just standing on the soil and being in my feet centers me in calm.

I close my eyes and visualize the truth that so often slips away, one author Michael Singer speaks of often: Every day we are all standing on a planet spinning through space in a universe that goes on forever. Why not enjoy the ride?

And the scenery.

Nature is God's masterpiece, from the acorn to the zebra, from the platypus to the stingray, from the Pacific Ocean to the nearest puddle.

You are part of that masterpiece, too. You are made of the same sacred stuff that makes up the sea, sand, and stars. We are all stardust.

When news of the world overwhelms me, nature soothes me, every time. Step away from the phone, the TV, the news, and be in your feet, right where they land on this grand planet. My friend Sherrie constantly tells me, "Be in your feet."

I try to get out every morning and ground myself on the Earth, to stand intentionally on this beautiful planet and absorb its energy. I breathe in its aroma, the dirt, the mud, the grass. This is our Magic Kingdom. Right here. Right now. No matter what the weather, I go outside before bed, scan the sky, and thank my lucky stars for getting another day on the best planet in the known universe.

Embrace a slice of nature every day. And if it rains or snows, savor it even more.

Question

What would it take today to see myself as a marvel and a masterpiece?

Affirmation

Nature is proof of how much God loves me.

Action

I will take one hour this week to fully embrace nature. I will hug a tree, walk barefoot, and smell the flowers.

Discovery

Here are my favorite sacred spots on Earth, and why . . .

Pamper

You deserve to be taken care of by somebody, and that somebody is you.

I love my feet.

I know, most people think feet are too ugly or gross to look at.

Not really. If they are ugly, it's only because we neglect those parts of ourselves that we don't find beautiful. I used to neglect mine. As a child, I went barefoot and ended the day with filthy feet. That's probably where I started the practice of washing my feet every single day. It's also a beautiful biblical moment in the story where Jesus washes the feet of his followers as an act of love.

My act of love for me is to pamper my feet every single day. I bought a stack of fluffy white washcloths, and every night I scrub my feet with a clean washcloth doused in rosemary mint soap. Then I dry my feet gently, massage lotion into them, crawl into bed, dab essential oil on the sole of each foot, put on clean socks because I'm always cold in bed, then elevate them on a pillow.

It's a simple routine, but it reminds me to pamper myself even if no one else does. It's my way to love me, even the parts that aren't always the most beautiful.

Question

What part of my body most needs pampered today?

Affirmation

I love my body, every sacred inch of it.

Action

Add a new pampering routine to your morning or evening.

Discovery

I am replenished and renewed every time I . . .

Abundance

Believe in abundance for you and everyone else.

Money scares most people. Some people say they want to have more money, yet they also resent "those people" who have lots of money. With 11 kids in our family, money was tight. The only people we were allowed to look down on were the ones that had money.

Too many people treat the word *rich* like a dirty word. To them, rich people are bad or greedy or lucky. The world was divided into two parts: the haves and the have none.

We were the have-nots. Only we really weren't. We always had everything we needed; we just didn't have most of what we wanted.

My thinking about money kept me stuck. I didn't feel worthy of money or wealth or nice things. Shame kept me from attracting them. The words *rich* and *money* felt unholy. I didn't want to become "those" people.

What about abundance?

That word felt right. I believe there is abundant love and goodness to go around for everybody. Money simply allows you to have more choices and to be more generous. Once I started to believe I was worthy of abundance, it flowed into my life.

An abundant life is one that is so rich, you love sharing all you have with others.

Question

How am I resisting abundance coming into my life today?

Affirmation

I am God's beloved rich child. I have a right to an abundant life right now.

Action

Collect all the money you can find, all that change from your coat pockets, purse, wallet, couch cushions, car seat, and floor, and set it in a sacred spot. Then give thanks for all the abundance you already have. Start small.

Discovery

I am a ready for all these dreams to come true . . .

....

....

....

....

....

....

....

....

....

....

....

....

....

Laugh

Don't take yourself so seriously. No one else does.

Laughter takes the punch right out of shame. Leave the bathroom with toilet paper on your shoes? Be the first to laugh. Drop a jar of pickles in the grocery store? You just found yourself in a pickle, so laugh.

Even during cancer treatments, laughter helped heal me. We survivors call it tumor humor. When my hair fell out from chemo, instead of feeling demoralized, I would grab a clump and tell the person next to me, "I'm so frustrated, you're making my hair fall out!" Then we both laughed.

Right now, stop everything and laugh.

Come on, you can do better than that.

Laugh a little louder. Laugh a little longer.

Laughter truly is the best medicine. During recovery from radiation and chemotherapy, I watched comedies to lift my spirits. When you laugh so hard that tears run down your face, you forget that you're bald.

The famous comedian Milton Berle once said, "Laughter is an instant vacation."

And it's a free one, so take it.

Question

What would happen today if I didn't take life so seriously?

Affirmation

Every moment life offers me the chance to laugh. I will take it!

Action

I will make a list of ten top comedies and watch one this week with someone who always makes me laugh.

Discovery

The last time I laughed so hard I nearly wet my pants . . .

Peace

To be a channel of peace, you have to keep your heart open.

Peace. Say the word softly and slowly, and you actually feel at peace.

Peace doesn't mean nothing bad is going on in your life. It doesn't mean everything stays calm all the time. It doesn't even mean the absence of being at war with anyone.

True peace is found in that quiet place within. It's a calm that doesn't depend on what anyone else says or does or thinks about us.

It's that peace that surpasses all understanding, a peace the world can't give or take away. The best way to find it is to pause and breathe it in, especially when the world around you is in turmoil.

On retreat I discovered this song by Carey Landry a great comfort: "Peace is flowing like a river, flowing out of you and me, flowing out into the desert, setting all the captives free."

Let go of what troubles you and fall into peace. Be like a leaf that simply bounces along the waves, without any resistance, floating past the chaos to find calm waters.

Question

What is troubling my heart right now?

Affirmation

Peace is an inside job. It is a gift that I can give myself right here, right now.

Action

At the end of each day, empty all your fears and troubles into a journal, then place your hand over them, surrender them, and give tomorrow a clean slate.

Discovery

The times in my life when I felt the greatest peace were . . .

....

....

....

....

....

....

....

....

....

....

....

....

....

Resilience

Don't quit before the miracle happens.

We humans are made of strong stuff. You have inside you the DNA of heroes and heroines. You are your ancestors' greatest dreams.

How many times have you bounced back from adversity? Come back from troubles? Rebooted your life and reinvented yourself?

If you don't evolve, you die. It's true of every species. Life happens *for* you, not *to* you, to foster the evolution of your soul.

Life can be hard, but you can do hard. During tough times, remind yourself how resilient you are. You are tougher than whatever has happened to you or will happen to you or is happening to you right now.

The resiliency of my parents fortifies me during tough times. My dad's family lost everything in the Great Depression. During

World War II, my dad left his small town in Ohio and flew 38 missions as a tail gunner over Burma to help save the world. My mom's brother Chuck ended up in a prisoner of war camp in Germany for three years. Her brother Michael survived the Dieppe Raid. They believed in spite of it all and made it home to enjoy the miracles that freedom gives.

If we have it in us to survive that kind of adversity, we can surely handle the small stuff.

Question

What is my personal superpower that makes me so resilient?

Affirmation

I can handle anything when I believe it is happening for me, not to me.

Action

Scan your body and thank the strongest parts of it.

Discovery

Here are five things I've overcome in life that remind me how resilient I already am . . .

Pause

Silence the noise.
In times of doubt or indecision,
be still and make room for God.

Sit down at a piano and bang on the keys. That's noise. Now hit the notes and pause between them. That's music.

The music of your life needs more pauses.

My friends in recovery taught me the power of the pause with these words from their book, *Twelve Steps and Twelve Traditions:* "In all times of emotional disturbance or indecision, we can pause, ask for quiet, and in the stillness simply say, 'God grant me the serenity to accept the things I cannot change, courage to change the things I can, and wisdom to know the difference.'"

Who doesn't need a bit more calm and stillness? I know I do. I love those simple words from Psalm 46:10 that read "Be still and know that I am God." I once saw a sign break it down: *Be still and know that I am. Be still and know. Be still. Be.*

Too often I find myself reacting to life instead of responding to it. My friends remind me often to pause, pray, then proceed.

Many days a little tug on my heart tells me to pause, place my hand on my heart, and remember there is one who has all power, and it isn't me.

What a relief.

Question

Where do I need to slow down in my day and hit the pause button?

Affirmation

Every time I pause, peace enters my life.

Action

I will create moments to pause through the day to check in with myself and get calm. I will set a timer on my phone to pause at least three times today.

Discovery

Here is my permission slip to silence the noise in my life . . .

....

....

....

....

....

....

....

....

....

....

....

....

....

Inspire

Find your holy grail.
Be who God meant you to be, and you will set the world on fire.

Two note cards inspire me every day.

One is a small card I keep near my computer that defines the word *inspire* this way:

1. To affect, guide, or arouse by divine influence.
2. To fill with enlivening or exalting emotion.
3. To stimulate to action, motivate; to affect or touch.

Then there's the Steve Jobs quote in my medicine closet that I read every single morning when I reach for my toothbrush: "If today were the last day of my life, would I want to do what I'm about to do today?"

I pause to make sure my answer is *Yes!* before I start my day.

Both cards remind me not to get caught up in petty gossip or grudges or complaints. I'm here to complete a sacred mission.

So are you.

To be inspired is to be in spirit, to be one with. It comes from the Latin word *inspirare*, to blow into, to breathe life into.

Today, breathe some life into your life. Be inspired to live a life from your spirit.

Question

What is my heroic mission on Earth today?

Affirmation

Today I will make something possible.

Action

Find a vacant lot or field and stand under the stars and scream your holy Yes! *to the Universe so loudly that the stars hear you.*

Discovery

This is what it would look like to truly live the holy assignment I've been given here on Earth . . .

Gratitude

Envy is a waste of time.
You already have
everything you need.

A little Amish guy I met 40 years ago used to ask himself at the end of each day, "How grateful am I?"

Mose Yoder taught me to pray for a "grateful, humble heart."

He also taught me that when you feel gratitude, you won't feel sad or lonely or envious. You feel whole and satisfied and at peace.

My friend Kathy taught me way back in 1980 to write down three things every day that I was grateful for to build up gratitude muscles.

At the end of each day, I write down the gifts life gives me. Moments of grace, things I didn't earn and don't deserve, those unexpected smiles from God that land on your heart.

Take a moment and list the everyday saints in your life: those people who make you feel grateful just knowing they are in this world. It could be famous people or strangers in your life, the cab driver who makes you smile, the security guard who makes you feel safe, or that heavenly host of others who have passed on, whose love still fills your heart with gratitude.

Question

What would it feel like to be grateful for it all?

Affirmation

No matter what happens or doesn't happen today, I am grateful for this great abundant life.

Action

Find three people you are grateful for and thank them in person for the gift of their being in your life.

Discovery

If I scanned my life for what I'm most grateful for, my Top Ten List would include . . .

....

....

....

....

....

....

....

....

....

....

....

....

....

Shine

Even if you feel invisible, your work and your worth aren't.

It's embarrassing to admit, but *Barbie* challenged me to shine brighter.

Yes, the movie named after America's favorite doll turned up the wattage of my life.

My two granddaughters played one of the songs from the movie and, as they sang along, the end of the song stuck with me. The lyrics address those fears we all have about standing out too much, about backing down too often out of fear, about how we will feel if we stand up and stand out and people turn away when they see who we really are.

What if we lose our courage? Our very breath? What if our moment to walk on stage happens and when the curtain is pulled back, we trip? We fall? We fail?

The song asks: "Or tonight, just tonight, what if I shine?"

What would happen if you did shine? The entire world would glow a little brighter.

It doesn't even take that much effort. The stars never complain that there's no room to shine or that it's too dark or too cold or that the moon is hogging the spotlight. They just shine.

Try it. Be your brightest self and surprise everyone, even you.

Question

What would it feel like to truly shine my light?

Affirmation

I am stardust. I was made to shine.

Action

Stand in a sunbeam of light. Spend five minutes feeling the warmth of the sun to refill your tank of stardust so you can shine brighter today.

Discovery

This is what keeps me from shining my light on the world . . .

No one else is in charge of your happiness. You are the CEO of your joy.

The Bible says that weeping may endure for a night, but joy comes in the morning.

It also says that God will turn our mourning into dancing.

God wants us to experience joy. To know a new freedom and a new happiness, to experience a new sense of inner freedom that leads us to more joy.

I used to have a bogeyman God who scared me. His main goal was to make demands of me and punish me now and at the end of my life with hellfire.

Not anymore. Every day, as the psalmist wrote, "I come to the altar of God, the God of my joy."

I decided to make a promise, a vow to myself, to choose joy. Every day I go looking for it. Joy isn't just something that happens to you; it's a stance you take in life.

Decide to live on the joyful side of life.

The poet Mary Oliver taught me that joy is not a crumb. It's the whole cake—à la mode.

Question

Who are the most joyful people in my life today, and what keeps me from spending more time with them?

Affirmation

God wants me to be happy now. Joy is my birthright.

Action

Take a video of yourself or a selfie and smile your most joyous smile.

Discovery

If I saw my life as one big joyride with a full tank of freedom, here's where my life would take me . . .

Awe

Life is always waiting to surprise you. Let it.

When we were little and got bored, we would walk through the house holding a small mirror pointed to the ceiling, which to us seemed like a brand-new world.

It felt like we were walking on a different planet, stepping over invisible steps that were really the doorways above us. We just wanted our boring old house to feel exciting and new. We never moved from that address, but every time we walked around with that mirror, our perception of our home shifted and surprised us.

Let life surprise you. There isn't a day when the world isn't brand new. The same goes for you. Every day you wake up, greet the world as if you've never been in this body on this planet in this home.

When you wake up, see everything with new eyes, hear with new ears, taste with new buds as if you just arrived on Earth. Be a pioneer.

Be in awe of every rock and leaf and bug, just like a child.

It's time to rediscover the world and see it through the eyes of awe.

Question

What would it take to trust life to surprise me with awe?

Affirmation

I experience awe every time I am willing to open my eyes and heart to it.

Action

For one hour, pretend you just arrived on Earth and explore everything as if you've never seen, heard, touched, or tasted it.

Discovery

If I stuffed my eyes with wonder, I would see . . .

....

....

....

....

....

....

....

....

....

....

....

....

....

Sleep

Get a good night's sleep. It might be the only time God has your full attention.

If you're like me, you still feel like a kid at night. I rarely want to go to bed, even when I'm tired. I don't want to miss anything.

Instead, I miss out on precious sleep. I end up staying up long past the point of exhaustion some nights. I'm trying to see tucking myself in early as a gift to myself, to my body, and to my soul.

Sleep is vital to the health of your brain. You wouldn't leave your phone battery to drain or your computer unplugged and expect it to work. You wouldn't drive your car on empty, yet I drive the car that is my body on empty way too often.

Sleep is also the place where we aren't resisting the inner calling that we shush while we're awake. Angels whisper in our ears all day, but we're too busy or our mind is too noisy to hear.

At night, it's our time to listen and be led to higher ground. Tonight, close your eyes and keep your ears open to hear the whispers of angels.

Question

What is keeping me from getting a good night's sleep every night?

Affirmation

I give my body and soul the gift of rest to renew every part of me.

Action

I will give myself an extra 15 minutes of sleep every day this week.

Discovery

If I were an angel, here's what would I whisper into my own ears as I fell asleep . . .

....

....

....

....

....

....

....

....

....

....

....

....

....

Faith

When you have nothing but faith, you have enough.

It's easy to believe when you have proof, but that isn't faith.

It's easy to believe when everything is going the way you want it to, but that isn't faith.

Faith is believing without proof, without any evidence at all, without any concrete clues that all is as it should be.

Faith also means waiting. I love what a friend recently told me: "God might not be early, but God is never late." If you trust God, then trust God's timing, which is almost always way past the point when we want things to change.

And if you can't trust the God you have, get a bigger, better God, one who loves you to the moon and back, like mine does.

It's hard to have faith in a God whose job description includes sending hellfire and brimstone. It's a lot easier to have faith in a God whose very identity is Love.

If you don't have that kind of God, borrow mine.

Question

What kind of God do I believe in?

Affirmation

Today, I choose faith, a faith that makes me fearless.

Action

I will write down three people who can give my faith a boost of rocket fuel and make plans this week to connect with them.

Discovery

Here's what it would it take to truly turn my life and will over to the care of a Higher Power . . .

Courage

No matter how you feel, get up, dress up, and show up for life.

Courage is defined as having mental or moral strength in the face of fear, grief, sadness, or pain.

I like this definition better: *Courage is when you're the only one who knows you're afraid.*

Some days I still feel like such a coward, but I no longer let fear stop me from writing or speaking up or living my most vibrant life.

If you want to have more courage, stretch your courage vocal cords by speaking up for someone else this week.

If you need to, pound your chest like a gorilla and, as Walt Whitman said, sound your "barbaric yawp," then go conquer the world, or at least your corner of it.

If you struggle with finding the energy or willpower to get out of bed and face another day, just count down like Mel Robbins does using her five-second launch into life: *five . . . four . . . three . . . two . . . one . . . UP!*

Just get up, dress up, and show up. And never give up.

Question

What fear am I willing to surrender this week?

Affirmation

I have all the courage I need right now to face everything in front of me.

Action

I will give fear an expiration date this week and write it out on a card to help me stop being afraid.

Discovery

If released forever all the fears that keep me stuck, this is how I would soar . . .

Beauty

Make peace with your body.
Every scar and mole, every wrinkle
and stretch mark, every extra
pound or pimple is a beauty
mark from a life well lived.

Look in the mirror. What do you see?

Fat? Freckles? Flab? Wrinkles? Moles? Scars? Stretch marks? Age spots?

Those aren't flaws; those are beauty marks. All of them.

Take a deep breath and take them all in. See yourself with new eyes.

What if we saw ourselves the way our Creator saw us? As an original masterpiece. As a being of infinite beauty. An earthly vessel for pure grace. The essence and embodiment of the deepest love in human form.

It's hard to do that when you start judging your body every morning and go on a scavenger hunt looking for flaws. As I aged, the brown spots on the back of my hands grew. I tried to cover them up with makeup. I decided to make peace with them. I call my age spots constellations. Those giant brown spots all over the back of my hands are clusters of stars. Look, there's Orion! And Pegasus!

They say that "beauty is in the eye of the beholder," so make sure it's in your eyes when you gaze at yourself because you are a beauty to behold.

Question

What is my most beautiful quality?

Affirmation

I am ready and willing to love all of me because I am a masterpiece, an original, one-of-a-kind, priceless work of art.

Action

Get naked and bless your body. Make peace with every sacred inch of it. Pause and thank all those beauty marks you earned from a life well lived.

Discovery

I forgive myself for neglecting and punishing my body. From now on I will love my body better by . . .

Acceptance

When you don't get what you want, you get something better. Experience.

My friends in recovery taught me that acceptance is the answer to everything. My job is to love what is, just as it is. It's not easy when life doesn't go my way. But I'm learning that my way isn't often what's best for me or for those I love.

Life doesn't happen to me; it just happens. I need to stop taking it personally. It's not raining because I planned an outdoor birthday party. It's raining because the clouds needed to release all that moisture.

The key to happiness is to live life on life's terms, not on my terms.

I don't always get what I want, and that's often a good thing. Life gives me something bigger and better and deeper and much more interesting than what I would have chosen.

Acceptance isn't easy. Sometimes it's hardest to accept and love ourselves as is. That's the place to start. God doesn't ask us to create a "new and improved" version of us. We were already made perfect.

Acceptance means we simply say, "Thank You for what is." No matter what is.

Question

What would change my life for the better today if I just accepted it and stopped arm wrestling it?

Affirmation

I accept and love living life exactly the way life unfolds today.

Action

I will practice saying thank you every day for what is without judging it.

Discovery

To live a joyful life of radical acceptance, I am willing to give up . . .

....

....

....

....

....

....

....

....

....

....

....

....

....

Smile

Tell your face to say thanks.

The best way to improve the way you look is to smile.

There's a line from the musical *Annie* that I just love: "You're never fully dressed without a smile." Too many of us forget to put one on, but it's the most beautiful thing we can wear.

Sometimes I feel happy inside, but the joy hasn't made its way to my face. I pass a mirror and see a woman hunched over, about to cave in on myself. No way, I remind myself. Then I flash a grin at that lady in the mirror to let her and life know I'm still in the game.

A smile communicates joy and love, comfort and calm. It's the same in every language. A smile is an international message that says, "Bring on the joy!"

Smile bigger and brighter. Make it 100-watt.

Not feeling it? Then look in the mirror and ask, "Self, do you want to be happy? What is the payoff for being miserable?" Misery loves company, but I hear joy throws bigger parties. Leave your pity party and join a real party. It's been said that you can choose to be happy or choose to be miserable. It takes the same amount of effort.

Start by smiling in the mirror. It's your ticket to the party called Life.

Question

What can I smile about right now?

Action

Smile your biggest smile every time you pass a mirror and high-five yourself.

Affirmation

I am the face of God to someone every time I smile.

Discovery

The last time I smiled so much my face hurt . . .

Music

Every great life needs a soundtrack, including yours.

Movies are so much better with music. Music adds drama, humor, and hope. Music creates momentum that carries the plot along and magnifies that moment of triumph at the end.

If you had a soundtrack to the movie that is your life, what music would you pick?

I created a "Joy" playlist on Spotify that includes "Margaritaville," "Girl on Fire," "Shut Up and Dance," "Red Solo Cup," "Brown Eyed Girl," "Surfin' USA," "Live Like You Were Dying," "Fame," "Walking on Sunshine," "Tequila Makes Her Clothes Fall Off," "Here for a Good Time," and "No Shoes, No Shirt, No Problem." All songs that make me smile and sing along.

Add a little more music to every day. Sing yourself to sleep. Listen to a childhood song. Crank up some opera in the shower and sing with it.

Learn one tune on the piano, ukulele, or harmonica. I taught myself Billy Joel's "Piano Man" and carry a harmonica in my car so I can play along when it comes on the radio.

Plato was right: "Music gives a soul to the universe, wings to the mind, flight to the imagination, and life to everything."

Question

In what part of my day do I need to listen to music most of all?

Affirmation

Music is a gift I deserve to give myself.

Action

I will create a new playlist of joy and add more music to my life every day.

Discovery

If I were truly living my joy, these songs would play on the soundtrack to my life . . .

Create

Create a life you love out of the life you have.

We are all artists called to create something with our lives. We're also called to create our lives, to transform all the material we've been given into a work of art.

You were given a unique set of talents and passions and experiences no one else in this world has. Consider all of that to be your paint, your brushes, your canvas, your unique supplies, to create a life of your dreams.

It's never too late to embrace your inner artist.

You can create a work of art in your kitchen, baking bread or pies or cookies. You can create a work of art by picking up your pen or sitting at your keyboard and setting your fingers free to fly and write a novel, a play, or one perfect poem.

You can create a work of art in how you arrange the books on your shelves, the flowers in a vase, or in how you love the child you are raising or the one living next door.

Create a new you by creating a new sacred morning routine. Include a few minutes for prayer, yoga, and meditation. Create a sacred evening routine, give thanks for the day, and write down the happiest moment to savor.

Your entire life is your art.

Question

What one thing can I change in my daily routine to create more?

Affirmation

My entire life is my masterpiece.

Action

Draw a picture of something that brings you peace.

Discovery

Here's what I am being called to create—and what is stopping me from doing it . . .

Stop

Even God took off a day to rest.

Some days it seems like the whole world is spinning way too fast.

The to-do list is too many pages long. The calendar has no room for you. The pressure to do everything and to do it right is overwhelming. The needs of everyone else are crushing. You feel like it is up to you to steer everything and everyone else's life in the right direction.

It's time to hit the brakes before you crash. Just stop. That's why cars have brakes: to keep them from crashing.

Use your brakes. Give yourself a time-out. Or a time to go inward.

For a few minutes, do nothing but breathe slowly. The world is still turning without you at the wheel. It's not going to crash if you get out of the driver's seat.

Right now, tell yourself, *I don't do stress. Not anymore.*

Schedule a day off just for you. Even God rested on the seventh day. The more you schedule in rest, the smoother your life will flow.

When you stop, you give yourself the gift of time. You create a buffer, a gentle pillow of space between you and the world.

Question

What is one thing I can stop doing that will bring me the greatest peace?

Affirmation

I am ready and willing to allow more peace to flow in.

Action

List everything you do in one day. Then go over that list and delegate five things and delete six. You are a human being, not a human doing.

Discovery

There are so many ways to say No. *I'm going to practice saying* No *to . . .*

....

....

....

....

....

....

....

....

....

....

....

....

....

Stars

You are stardust.
It's in your DNA to shine.

It's hard to believe, but it's true: We are all made of stardust.

If we all really believed that, why don't we all shine brighter? Why are we afraid to sparkle?

It is our light, our talents, our gifts that often scare us the most, not our insecurities. God gave those gifts to us to use, not to hide under a bushel.

You are already special just by the nature of your being. You don't have to prove your worth. You were born worthy. If your light is too much for others, don't dim it. Don't diminish you to fit in. Don't waste your wattage on those who want to cower in the dark, too afraid of life to fully live it.

I have a mug on my desk that reminds me to Glow Up! I also keep a greeting card covered in stars with a quote from Walt

Whitman: *Let your soul stand cool and composed before a million universes.*

Don't just look at the stars; remember that you are one. Be human glitter. Shower joy confetti all over your life and never let anyone keep you from shining.

Question

What would my star name be?

Affirmation

I am stardust and the Universe loves how I sparkle.

Action

Dance under the stars and make a wish on the brightest one you see.

Discovery

I possess so many talents and gifts. These are the ones that scare me the most . . .

....

....

....

....

....

....

....

....

....

....

....

....

....

Yes

The world needs your *Yes!*

Say *Yes!* to *you* this week. A loud, bold *yes*, not a timid, shy, mousy one.

We're so busy giving ourselves away and saying yes to everyone else, it's time to give ourselves a bold, vibrant, loud *Yes!*

Say *Yes!* to bubble baths. Say *Yes!* to pedicures. Say *Yes!* to going to bed early or sleeping in longer. Say *Yes!* to a massage or a bowl of ice cream or both.

Make your life feel like a pleasure cruise with a spa, flower shop, all-you-can-eat buffet, and a grand view of every starry sky.

Say *Yes!* to a day at the art museum. Say *Yes!* to standing under a waterfall. Say *Yes!* to every inch of your body screaming to be loved.

Saying *Yes!* to you might mean saying *No* to all the things the world is asking of you. You are allowed to say *No*, so you can say *Yes!*

I just gave you permission. Use your holy *No* to embrace your holier *Yes!*

Question

What can I say Yes! *to today?*

Affirmation

I am a bold, human exclamation mark who says Yes! *to life.*

Action

I will write the word Yes! *on my mirror in lipstick or on sticky notes I put near my toothbrush, doorway, and dashboard as a reminder to practice saying* Yes! *to me all week.*

Discovery

These are things and people and plans and dreams that I am ready to say Yes! *to . . .*

....

....

....

....

....

....

....

....

....

....

....

....

....

Reward

Make each day a slice of heaven—à la mode.

I no longer expect other people to celebrate me or fill me up with love.

I used to put that burden on others, yet I rarely told them exactly what I needed or wanted because I didn't even know what I needed or wanted.

I no longer wait for someone else to compliment me. I try not to count how many *likes* or *shares* my social media posts get. It's time for me to celebrate myself.

Every day, I give myself a little reward. A treat. A poem. A bubble bath. I keep a stash of chocolate peppermints from Trader Joe's just for me. Yes, it's a private stash no one else gets. My friend Derdriu buys herself fresh flowers every Monday. I love that!

Give yourself a reward just for making it through another day.

Reward yourself with something that feeds your body, mind, heart, and soul. A beautiful poem by Mary Oliver. A song that makes your heart sing. A delicious bite of chocolate. The sweetest nectarine or clementine you can find.

Stand in the mirror and praise yourself. Give yourself a pat on the back. High-five yourself in the mirror. Say your name in a loving way. Tell yourself how much you love you.

You—yes, you—are a reward!

Question

What reward is my soul craving?

Affirmation

I am worth celebrating.

Action

Every day I will give myself a reward just for being my bold, beautiful, brave self.

Discovery

I'm going to celebrate life and reward myself every day by adding this to my life . . .

Empty

Empty yourself of all desires and love what *is*.

It sounds like a contradiction, but if you want your life to be full of love, you have to be empty of all desires, all demands, all conditions you put on life.

A friend once challenged me to love life unconditionally. No struggle, just surrender. No asserting my will on anything. Just surrendering to what is.

The mystics experience God in everything and experience God in the nothing, in the grand emptiness. Maybe our natural state is to be empty.

When I first set eyes on the Grand Canyon and faced that magnificent hole, instead of being filled with awe, I was emptied by awe. That great, grand nothingness left me silent, stunned, and absolutely hollow inside. Something that magnificent should have echoed a grand chorus of hallelujahs, yet it was completely still.

Imagine the beautiful space inside us if we allowed ourselves to be emptied of negativity. Empty of the unhappy stories we tell ourselves. Empty of the grudges we keep. Empty of the fears we constantly nurture.

There is a grand canyon within us, a hollow, holy space that only God can fill. As St. Augustine said, “Thou hast formed us for Thyself and our hearts are restless until they rest in Thee.”

When we rest in that empty space, then God or the Universe or the Source of All Being that is Love and Light and Perfect Joy can fill us up with something better.

Something we’ve been seeking all along.

Question

What inner clutter keeps me from being at peace?

Affirmation

I am wide open and ready to receive more Love.

Action

Release a hostage from your life. Pick one person you have closed your heart on and set them—and you—free.

Discovery

I want my house or life or relationships or soul to look and feel like this after I declutter it . . .

....

....

....

....

....

....

....

....

....

....

....

....

....

Hope

Harness the power of hope.

The world can weigh you down with all its turmoil and strife. Some days life just shatters you into a million pieces.

I spend a lot of time in nature because nature never loses hope. Nature knows the best is yet to come. Nature is always coming back to life. In winter, the trees look dead, but all that new life is just sleeping under the bark until spring.

Hope had a new meaning after I read the book *Faith, Hope and Carnage* by Australian musician Nick Cave. The greatest line from the book was this: "Optimism is hope with a broken heart."

It still takes my breath away. Cave lost his son, Arthur, in 2015. Arthur was just 15 when he fell off a cliff and died after experimenting with LSD for the first time. How did Cave go on?

"I don't think strength has much to do with anything," he wrote. "It seems to me that you just take the next least-wounding step."

The next *least-wounding* step. My heart gasped reading that.

In time he saw grief as a positive force. It gave him a reckless energy, a feeling of invincibility, and "a sort of fearless abandonment to destiny."

Does it ever get better? Yes, he wrote, "We become different. We become better."

What gives me hope? Caterpillars. Puppies. Pregnant women. Giggling brides. Kind strangers. People who vote. Babies. Pennies in a fountain. A blank page in a journal. Every single sunrise.

And people like you.

Question

What is my greatest hope for the world today?

Affirmation

I will hope for the best and love what unfolds in this day.

Action

List five steps that could turn your greatest hope into reality, and take the first step today.

Discovery

One time when life got better in spite of it all was . . .

Receive

Giving gifts is admirable, but receiving is a gift, too.

I suck at receiving.

Giving comes naturally, but receiving makes me uncomfortable.

Often, as I'm saying thank you for a gift, I'm already thinking about who needs or wants the gift more than I do.

It's not because I'm so giving or good hearted. It's because I sometimes don't feel worthy enough to receive a gift.

I skipped over receiving because, somewhere deep inside, I didn't feel worthy of those earrings or that gift card or those flowers. When you're hungry for love for too long, you can get too comfortable with the hunger and not know what to do when food comes your way.

Now on my birthday, I soak up the texts. I savor the words each person wrote. I embrace the physical gifts. I read every card twice. I inhale the roses, caress the daisy petals, bury my face in the bouquet as if it were a pillow.

When you receive a gift, you give a gift to the giver and yourself. Whether you realize it or not, you are a gift to this world and to the person who just gave you that gift.

Celebrate yourself with something that feeds your body, mind, heart, and soul. A beautiful poem. A song that makes your heart sing. A delicious bite of chocolate. Say your name in a loving way and tell yourself how much you are loved.

God already gave you the perfect gift: You. It's time to receive it.

Question

What's the best gift I can give myself?

Affirmation

Today I will receive love in every form because I am worth celebrating.

Action

Every day I will place my hands over my heart and give thanks for the gift of me.

Discovery

I am a gift to this world simply because . . .

....

....

....

....

....

....

....

....

....

....

....

....

....

See

The secret of life is no secret.
It is sprinkled all over your life.

Of the five senses we have, sight is the one I treasure the most.

Ever since third grade I needed eyeglasses. I couldn't make out anything more than three feet way.

When I got contact lenses at 21, the eye doctor had a sign in his office that I've never forgotten. It read, "Next to life itself, God's most precious gift is sight." I'd never even given it any thought until then.

I wore glasses, then contacts, then had my natural lenses replaced after getting cataracts. Now I can see 20/20 without any aid. What a miracle to open my eyes in the morning and see without glasses!

I can't imagine never seeing a sunset or a starry night or the ocean waves or the faces of all the people I love, yet how often do I lose sight of the beauty around me or take it for granted because I'm too busy or have my face buried in my cell phone? Pretty much daily.

There is also another way we see.

A beautiful French book, *The Little Prince*, offers this way: "And now here is my secret, a very simple secret: It is only with the heart that one can see rightly. What is essential is invisible to the eye."

Open the eyes of your heart and you will see better than 20/20.

Question

What have I missed seeing that is right in front of me?

Affirmation

I will keep my heart open today to see what is most essential.

Action

I will look on the world as if today is both my first day on Earth and my last.

Discovery

The secret to life is . . .

Kindness

Just be kind.
It isn't even that hard.

The world could sure use more kindness.

You can't change all the cruelties of the world or the political harshness or natural disasters all over the globe. You can't stop the wars and hate and injustices, but you can vow not to let them stop you from being kind right where you are.

All we can do is our part, but even our small part sends out wide ripples into the world. When you're kind, others will be kinder.

Make kindness your secret weapon. Turn kindness into your superpower. Before you say or do or think anything for too long, ask yourself: *Is this kind? Is this necessary? Is this useful? Does it add to the mercy and compassion of the world? Does it diminish anyone?*

Every day, do one random, radical, secret act of kindness for someone who needs it most. Make kindness contagious so it spreads around the world. It might just come back to greet you on a day when you need it most.

Question

What is the kindest thing I can say or do right now?

Affirmation

Kindness is my superpower.

Action

I will be kinder than necessary to all beings and commit five random acts of kindness and keep them anonymous.

Discovery

This is what keeps me from being kinder . . .

....

....

....

....

....

....

....

....

....

....

....

....

....

The best is yet to come.

I love the final words of Apple cofounder Steve Jobs. Before he died on Oct. 5, 2011, in his final moments, he looked at his family for a long time, then looked past them and said, "OH WOW. OH WOW. OH WOW."

It gives me goose bumps to think of what he must have seen.

When writer Anne Lamott picked three essential prayers as the title of one of her books, she chose *Help, Thanks, Wow*. God must love hearing those last two.

You are God's wow. Think about it: The Creator designed you, with all those unique quirks and talents, moles and freckles and pimples and pouches and surely must have said, WOW!

Yes, God danced on the day you were born. Or to paraphrase Shakespeare, "A star danced, and under that, you were born."

Embrace your wow. Be awed by it. Get out under those stars and remember that you, dear one, are made of stardust.

Question

What would it mean to fully and completely embrace your wow everywhere in your life today?

Affirmation

I am someone's wow!

Action

Wow someone else's world. Mail someone a gift card, a thank you, or a love note.

Discovery

I hope my last words are . . .

Special Thanks

Thanks for choosing this book and trusting it to guide you to your own treasure chest of wisdom. I hope it continues to bless your life long after you finish all 52 words.

I'm eternally blessed by all the great writers of the world whose words saved me, by all the best teachers and devoted friends and family members who have loved and supported me and my writing all my life.

Big thanks to my spiritual guide, Lynn McCown, who gives me clarity to see every detour as a spiritual adventure. Endless gratitude to my ninth-grade English teacher Sam Ricco, who helped me fall in love with words.

I'm most grateful to my publisher, David Gray at Gray & Company and his talented team, for bringing this book to life. Big thanks to copy editor Linda Cuckovich, who made every line sing and still sound like me. My friend Vicki Prussak gets a high-five for constantly cheering me on with her endless ideas and creativity.

To all my fans, friends, and followers on social media, thanks for reminding me of my mission. To booksellers and librarians everywhere, you are pillars of democracy. I pray that you stand tall for the next generation of readers.

I offer the deepest gratitude and love to my three children and their spouses, Gabrielle and James, Ben and Melanie, Joe and Sarah, and my huge family, Brett Nation, for loving me through one of the roughest years of my life.

Endless hugs to my sacred three, my perfect joy, my grandchildren Asher, Ainsley, and River. Their mom, my daughter Gabrielle, is my biggest miracle and my best friend, who reminds me every day how much I am loved.

And, as always, endless gratitude to the Source of it all, the God of my joy, for every single word and every single breath of life.

About the Author

Regina Brett is the author of the *New York Times* bestseller *God Never Blinks: 50 Lessons for Life's Little Detours,* which has been published in 24 languages.

She is also the author of *Little Detours and Spiritual Adventures*; *Be the Miracle: 50 Lessons for Making the Impossible Possible; God is Always Hiring: 50 Lessons for Finding Fulfilling Work*; and six more books exclusively published in Poland.

She became a journalist in 1986 and has been a newspaper columnist since 1994. She was twice named finalist for the Pulitzer Prize in Commentary. She writes a weekly column for the *Cleveland Jewish News* and for Little Detours with Regina Brett at reginabrett.substack.com.

Regina has a bachelor's degree in journalism and a master's degree in religious studies. She lives in Cleveland, Ohio, with her golden doodle, McIntyre.

ReginaBrett.com
Facebook: ReginaBrettFans
Instagram, X: @reginabrett